TEEN MENTAL HEALTH™

antisocial behavior

Frank Spalding

ROSEN
PUBLISHING®

New York

For George, Gowanus's own Lord Nelson.
May you find peace in a life at sea.

Published in 2012 by The Rosen Publishing Group, Inc.
29 East 21st Street, New York, NY 10010

Library of Congress Cataloging-in-Publication Data

Spalding, Frank.
Antisocial behavior / Frank Spalding.—1st ed.
    p. cm.—(Teen mental health)
Includes bibliographical references and index.
ISBN 978-1-4488-4585-9 (library binding)
1. Antisocial personality disorders. 2. Antisocial personality disorders—Prevention. 3. Conduct disorders in adolescence. I. Title.
RC555.S69 2011
616.85'82—dc22

2011000527

Manufactured in the United States of America

CPSIA Compliance Information: Batch #S11YA: For further information, contact Rosen Publishing, New York, New York, at 1-800-237-9932.

contents

chapter one

Antisocial Behavior During the Teen Years

According to a study conducted by the U.S. Department of Education, approximately one-third of American teens reported being harassed at school by their peers. The students doing the harassing often hide their antisocial behavior from school administrators and are never punished. For the students being harassed, however, it's a different story. They can feel alienated from their classmates, frightened, and

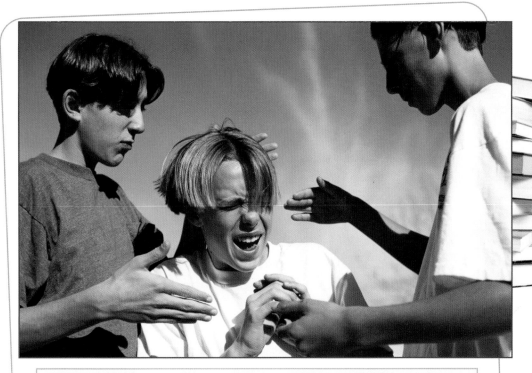

One of the most common forms of antisocial behavior in the teen years is bullying.

alone. Sometimes bullying and harassment can cross the line to threats or physical violence. When bullying and antisocial behavior go too far, it isn't just the victim who suffers. Kids who are found guilty of threatening behavior or assault can face serious consequences. And both those who are bullied and those who are bullying have been found to be less socially and psychologically adjusted as they develop into adults.

The teen years can be difficult for many young people. Some act out, displaying a number of antisocial and destructive behaviors without always fully grasping the consequences of their actions. Destructive activities such as drug and alcohol use, vandalism, theft, and harassment might seem like no big deal at the time, but they all can have long-term consequences. And of course, antisocial behavior can inflict long-lasting and serious damage on teen victims.

Young adults targeted by antisocial behavior may be unable to cope with the stress and may fall into deep depression. Some teens have, tragically, committed suicide as a result of abuse and harassment. In recent years, the negative effects of bullying and harassment among students have been scrutinized by the news media. The prevalence of electronic communications and social media has given rise to cyberbullying, which targets teens even when they are away from school. Today more than ever, teens need help dealing with antisocial behavior.

The teenage years are a time of establishing one's independence. It's common for teens to push back against authority and test boundaries. This is normal behavior for people to engage in on the road to adulthood. Rebellion is often exhilarating, and it gives many teens a feeling of courage and invincibility. The rush that comes from acting out can feel intoxicating—but it's dangerous. No one is invincible, and acting out can have serious consequences.

Few teens make it to adulthood without witnessing, being the victim of, or perpetrating some sort of antisocial behavior. It would be unrealistic to think that one can pass through the teenage years without being bullied or without being tempted to partake in antisocial behavior by one's peers. The good news, however, is that it is common for teens to become less antisocial as they grow and mature.

Crossing the Line

In 2010, Michigan assistant attorney general Andrew Shirvell spent months harassing Chris Armstrong, the first openly gay student body president of the University of Michigan. An alumnus of the University of Michigan, Shirvell seemed to have a problem with Armstrong and started a blog that was critical of him. Although he claimed he was simply exercising his First Amendment right of free speech, he went as far as to accuse Armstrong of being a Nazi and a racist. He even videotaped Armstrong's house, and harassed members of his family. Many people thought that Shirvell had crossed a line, and he was fired for his actions. Even though he was out of high school, Armstrong was still being bullied, this time by a grown man in a position of political power.

Curious teens often test the boundaries of what is considered to be acceptable behavior. But where is the line? When does pushing someone's buttons or causing mischief cross the line into antisocial behavior? Identifying and avoiding the point beyond which one's words or actions go too far is one of the most important tasks of the teen years. Pushing against boundaries and acting antisocially once in a while is one thing, but making a habit of it is quite another. Consistently threatening others, lying, stealing, and committing acts of violence or vandalism are not simply a normal part of growing up. Teens who commit these acts on a regular basis aren't just making mayhem. Rather, they are seriously disrupting their lives and the lives of others.

Antisocial behavior can take the form of taunting, gossiping, and emotional cruelty. Talking badly about someone or treating someone else as an outcast is every bit as harmful as physical violence.

Threats and Intimidation

Many teenagers feel that it's vitally important for them to fit in with their friends, and some teens will do almost anything to be accepted. Sometimes this means picking on other students to impress their peers or become popular. Some bullying takes place directly—the bully threatens or physically attacks the victim out in the open. School administrators are legally bound to prevent students from being assaulted by their peers.

Not all bullying is so obvious, however. For instance, some victims of bullying may never be physically attacked (avoided and treated like an outcast). Instead, they are socially isolated and ostracized by their peers. All teens crave acceptance, and the effects of this negative treatment can be devastating. Even students who want to be friends with the victim of this kind of bullying might be hesitant to reach out, afraid that they will receive the same sort of treatment. The aftermath of bullying can be very serious. The long-term psychological effects of continual torment can last long into adulthood.

Drug and Alcohol Use

Some adolescents experiment with drug, alcohol, and tobacco use. Besides being generally illegal, these activities can have extremely detrimental effects on one's health and well-being. The possession and sale of illegal drugs can lead teens into serious trouble, and drug and alcohol use frequently results in poor academic performance at school. In addition, substance abuse can impair one's judgment, leading to an

Teen drinking can lead to poor decision-making, alcohol poisoning, and drunk driving accidents and fatalities.

increased incidence of risk-taking, driving under the influence, unsafe sex, fighting, and other harmful behaviors.

Many substance-abusing teens may not feel that they are taking part in an antisocial activity, especially if they are drinking or doing drugs with others. Many of these people may be new acquaintances, sometimes even older kids. Entering a new social circle can be exciting, and a teen who falls into substance abuse may not notice at first that he or she is alienating his or her true friends and family members. It's good to remember that new friendships built on drug and alcohol abuse are seldom very strong, satisfying, or long-lived. These new friends might not care much about school or staying out of trouble. In fact, they probably aren't real friends at all.

Shoplifting is a crime. What starts as a dare or a lark may end in arrest, steep fines, and a criminal record.

Theft and Vandalism

Teenagers are predisposed to thrill-seeking behavior. Some get a thrill out of shoplifting or other forms of theft. Stealing something small might not seem like a big deal, but it is still wrong. Shoplifting

10

is a crime, and moreover, your theft could get other people, like store employees and managers, into trouble.

Other teens experiment with vandalism, try breaking and entering, or destroy others' property. Pulling a harmless prank once is one thing, but violating others' space or maliciously destroying their property is another. Once again, it's a thin line between youthful experimentation and illegal activity, between negative behavior and a serious behavioral problem.

Cyberbullying

Before the proliferation of personal computers, cell phones, and social networking sites such as Facebook, students who were bullied at school could look forward to returning home, where the bullies couldn't reach them. This is no longer the case, however. Now bullies can send their victims threatening messages and texts and can mock them online. In 2007, nine hundred thousand high school students reported that they had been cyberbullied.

The results of this antisocial behavior can be devastating, and teens who are relentlessly cyberbullied can feel hopeless. Since this kind of bullying takes place outside of school property, school officials can be powerless to exert their authority in order to stop it. It's best not to respond to messages from cyberbullies. In fact, it's best to not even bother opening them and reading them. Such messages should certainly never be forwarded to anyone else.

In addition, one of the surest ways to reduce the chance of being cyberbullied is to carefully safeguard one's private information. Private information includes one's phone number, e-mail address, physical address, birth date, and even photographs of oneself. And remember, if anyone directly threatens you with physical harm online, it's best to tell a trusted adult. Threats should always be taken seriously.

Targets of Antisocial Behavior

Antisocial behavior is seldom victimless. Targets of bullying often feel anxious and may have low self-esteem. They may drop out of extracurricular activities where they encounter bullies or may even skip school to avoid being victimized. Victims of bullying can become depressed,

While graffiti can be art and can demonstrate enormous talent and skill, it is illegal when done on public and private spaces without authorization.

perform poorly in school, and have a hard time sleeping. As a teenager, it can be difficult to look ahead into the future, when high school is over and one never has to see these bullies again. In some cases, students who have been targeted by bullies have gone as far as to inflict harm upon themselves. Some have even committed suicide.

Loved ones of those who turn to drugs and alcohol are forced to watch as their friends or family members grow distant, either lost in oblivion or off to spend time with a different social group. Once-familiar friends begin acting differently, and their personalities often change. Kids using drugs and alcohol generally do not realize the tremendous risks they are taking. Substance use can result in serious health problems, and some teens may not realize that they are at risk of becoming addicted until it is too late.

Other forms of petty crime can quickly result in serious penalties for those that commit them. It's possible to run out of second chances fairly quickly and suffer the legal consequences of one's actions. For instance, the prevalence of graffiti has increased over the last twenty years around the world. Mainly created by young people, the artistic merits of graffiti have long been argued over. Today, it has been fully accepted as valid by the mainstream art world. However, spray painting buildings and other public spaces is against the law, unless the area being painted has been officially set aside for graffiti and other forms of public art. In New York City, for example, there is an entire division of the police force that is dedicated to combating graffiti and identifying and arresting graffiti artists. No matter what the artistic merits are, graffiti is still considered vandalism, even if it is made with the best intentions.

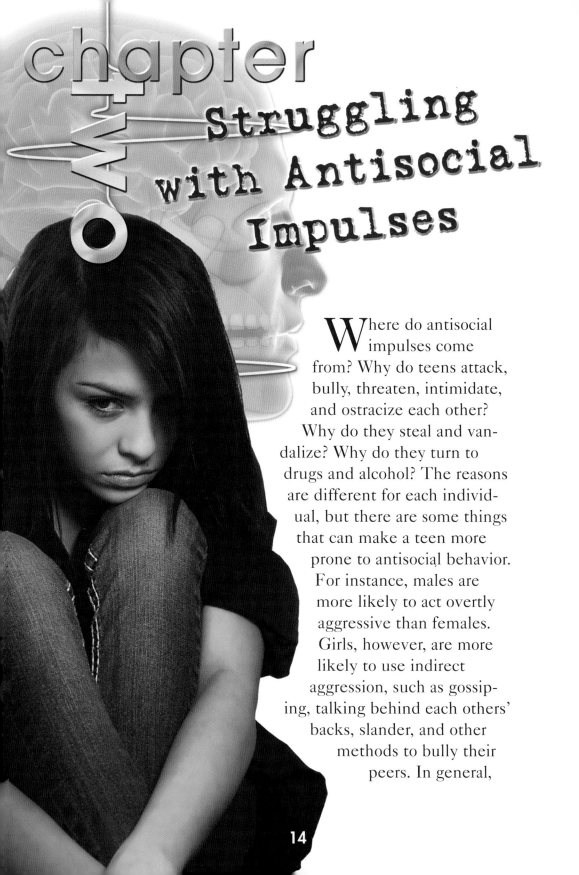

chapter Two

Struggling with Antisocial Impulses

Where do antisocial impulses come from? Why do teens attack, bully, threaten, intimidate, and ostracize each other? Why do they steal and vandalize? Why do they turn to drugs and alcohol? The reasons are different for each individual, but there are some things that can make a teen more prone to antisocial behavior. For instance, males are more likely to act overtly aggressive than females. Girls, however, are more likely to use indirect aggression, such as gossiping, talking behind each others' backs, slander, and other methods to bully their peers. In general, males are more likely to experience bullying, and this bullying mostly occurs with other males. Females, however, are more likely to experience bullying from both sexes.

The Roots of Antisocial Urges

As kids get older, they tend to become less antisocial. Learning how to ignore or transform antisocial impulses is a part of growing up. And having strong antisocial urges during the teen years doesn't necessarily mean that one will have to deal with them into adulthood. However, the teen years are an often confusing, frightening, and

Teasing, taunting, and ostracizing someone can create deep but often invisible wounds. Sometimes teens can become so victimized by antisocial behavior that they contemplate harming themselves.

anxiety-ridden time, increasing the likelihood of episodes of antisocial behavior.

Every kid who struggles with anger and frustration has a different story and a different set of challenges to overcome. Some teens become so worried that they will be singled out for poor treatment by their peers that they begin to see negativity all around them. They may see hostility where none exists, interpreting the most innocent words and gestures as insults, rejection, or mockery. It feels to them like the whole world is against them, and they want to strike back. Other teens have a difficult time getting along with classmates. When they act negatively toward classmates, their classmates become more reluctant to accept them. So they lash out at their classmates again, creating a vicious circle that leads to alienation and isolation. Frustration at school can lead to poor classroom performance and increased negative attention from teachers and school administrators.

Another major factor spurring antisocial behavior is the environment in which one is raised. Kids raised in neighborhoods with high levels of crime may be exposed to violence, drugs and alcohol, theft, vandalism, and other forms of antisocial behavior at an early age. Teens may receive mixed messages. On the one hand, they're told that violence, crime, and drug abuse is wrong, but on the other hand it seems normal in their environment. Teens in tough environments may find themselves in situations where taking the high road and doing the right thing is exceedingly difficult. According to a U.S. Department of Health and Human Services report, the most important predictor of whether or not teens will be involved in crime and violent behavior is if they have friends who are involved in gangs, crime, or other forms of antisocial activity.

Finally, one of the biggest influences on any teen is his or her family life. Children who bully are more likely to spend time at home without supervision. Aggression, abuse, or violence in the home has a profound effect on a child's behavior. In addition, an unstable home can mean that a teen may not be able to turn to his or her family with problems or concerns and may not be able to get advice to deal with issues at school. Kids who see violence at home are more prone to express their anger and frustration physically at school. Kids who hear cruel insults and bad words at home are more likely to get in trouble for talking back in class, swearing, badmouthing classmates, or verbally taunting other students.

To be sure, some people are simply more predisposed to antisocial behavior than others. However, it's important to remember that antisocial urges don't develop out of nowhere. They are borne out of complex social interactions, pressures, and circumstances. Bullying is a learned behavior, and often stems from an abusive or neglectful home environment. Everyone lives in the center of a massive social network, and they are influenced by everyone and everything in their orbit. That being said, no one is completely at the mercy of his or her circumstances. Everyone has the power of choice, no matter whom or what they are. Even if you can't control your circumstances, your family, your peers, or what goes on in your neighborhood, you still have the power to choose how you will behave.

Forcing yourself to engage in a cooling-off period when angry is essential. The goal is to calm oneself down to the point at which you can begin thinking more rationally.

The Physical Effects of Anger

When people get angry, the body goes through a number of physical changes. The heart beats faster, the body releases adrenaline, and all of the senses are heightened. This is often referred to as the fight-or-flight response. It is the body's response to a perceived threat—literally, it prepares someone to either fight off the threat or run from it. In modern civil society, there is little need for this instinct, but it persists nonetheless. When people get angry, they are prepared to defend themselves from a threat, no matter what they perceive it to be.

Taking Control

Since anger is difficult to control, you can't be blamed for what you do when you get mad, right? Wrong. Some people will say horrible things to people they care about when they're angry. When the anger wears off, they realize they didn't mean any of it. For the person who was the target of their aggression, however, these words still hurt, and the hurt lingers after the anger has passed.

It's easy for people to blame rash actions on their anger, especially if they are looking for an excuse to cross boundaries. No one starts a fight when completely calm. Instead, they ramp up their aggression by insulting the person they want to fight. They then push the other person. They may even get angry enough that they will break ordinary social codes of civility and restraint and actually hit another person. Think back to the last time you said something to someone that you later regretted. Ask your-self—were you angry when you said it? And if you could take it back, would you? Unfortunately, there's no way to go back in time and take back what has been said or done. The only way to avoid saying or doing something that you regret is to not say or do it in the first place. This involves learning how to control your anger or frustration and preventing it from boiling over.

There are a number of ways to bring oneself back from the brink of anger and unreason and to return to thinking calmly and logically. One simple way to do this is to take deep breaths and count to ten slowly when angry. This short cooling-down period is often enough to keep people from doing something that they will soon regret. You can also learn to avoid situations that typically make you extremely angry. Another strategy is to completely visualize the consequences of one's actions. For instance, what would be the consequences of spray painting graffiti on the side of a store? Some people might see the graffiti and think it was really cool. On the other hand, the person who owns the building would either be stuck with the graffiti or have to pay to paint over it or have it removed. Or think about the consequences of bullying a peer. Even if the bullying isn't physical, think of how terrible and ashamed he or she will feel and how you would never do the same thing to someone you cared about. Nor would you ever want to be on the receiving end of such bullying.

Beyond this, think about the consequences that you yourself might suffer. Besides getting in trouble in school, think about how people will perceive you if you do or say things that hurt others. People might act like they respect you, but do they really? Or are they just afraid to get on your bad side? It's also worth considering that, according to a study by the nonprofit organization Invest in Kids, about 60 percent of people who were bullies in grades six through nine were convicted of a crime by the time they were twenty-four years old.

Being Honest

Life is difficult for teenagers. Things move fast, and every teen is under unbelievable social and academic pressure. Feelings of frustration, sadness, rage, and other strong emotions are common. Personal circumstances and stress feed into this as well, and sometimes it feels like the only way to take control of everything is to act out. Whatever rewards you feel that you get from antisocial behavior, they are nothing compared to the costs.

Recognizing this and examining where one's antisocial behavior comes from is key to learning self-control. What makes you want to take your anger out on others? Is it because you have low self-esteem or because you are having conflicts with a parent? Anger can reveal itself in odd ways—sometimes people feel a disproportionate amount of anger over relatively minor things. Frustration can build up inside a person until he or she begins actively looking for an excuse to unload it on others. This isn't fair to others, and it isn't fair to you. Rather than passing on rage and anger to others, it's best to honestly examine the cause of these feelings and take responsibility for one's actions.

The Importance of Empathy

Empathy is the ability to recognize, and share in, another person's feelings. Having empathy can involve feeling angry on another person's behalf, feeling sad when they are in pain, and sharing in someone else's happiness. Human beings generally have well-developed senses of empathy, and this quality is widely regarded as setting humans apart from other animals.

As people age, the way that their brains work changes somewhat. A recent study undertaken at the London Institute of Cognitive Neuroscience indicated that teenagers use a different part of the brain than adults when considering other people's feelings. It is believed that people's sense of empathy is something that develops over time. Children generally first begin to understand that other people have feelings when in kindergarten.

Over the years, they continue to build their capacity to feel empathy for others.

In 2010, researchers from the University of Valencia came to the conclusion that the part of the brain responsible for empathy overlaps with the part of the brain responsible for aggression and violence. The researchers believe that if young people are taught to be more empathetic, it will be more difficult for them to act aggressively or violently toward others.

There are a number of prescription medications available for teens suffering from ADHD, depression, anxiety, and mood and behavior disorders.

Behavioral Disorders

Some young people have behavioral disorders that make them more disposed to antisocial behavior than others. Teens who have attention deficit/hyperactivity disorder (ADHD) may become frustrated in school, which can lead to them acting out. Teens with depression, mood disorders, and learning disorders face similar challenges.

People with oppositional defiant disorder (ODD) often act out continuously. ODD is evident in children at an early age, although it can be misdiagnosed as ADHD or any of a number of other disorders. Teens with ODD argue with adults and other authority figures, intentionally provoke their peers, act angry and vengeful at perceived slights or insults, and blame other people for their own behavior. Sometimes teens with severe ODD are given medication to help control their moods.

Some people who have what is called an antisocial personality disorder, an extremely serious chronic mental illness, often have difficulty respecting the feelings of others. Lacking a sense of empathy and with no ability to connect meaningfully with others, people with antisocial personality disorder exhibit aggressive behavior and frequently feel no remorse if they hurt other people. Going through life consistently lying and cheating others and unable to form lasting relationships, they often run into trouble with the law. Over time, people with this disorder can learn to cope with it, but when they are still young, they are much more likely to have difficulty functioning in society. Young people with antisocial personality disorder may exhibit extreme behaviors such as violence toward people and animals, arson, sexual assault, or compulsive lying.

For people diagnosed with these disorders, therapy—and sometimes medication—are generally recommended. There is no simple cure for these disorders, and the effectiveness of treatment can be unpredictable. Still, treatment is invaluable, and while its beneficial effects can be difficult to quantify, it can make a huge difference in the life one goes on to lead.

chapter three

When You're the Victim: Coping with the Effects of Antisocial Behavior

B eing the target of antisocial behavior can be a harrowing and profoundly isolating experience. Over time, it can lead to feelings of depression, helplessness, anger, and frustration. It can be hard to imagine a time when the torment will end. Even worse, it's often difficult to figure out the best way to respond to antisocial behavior.

What is the best course of action for dealing with a bully or an overly aggressive classmate? Sometimes telling a teacher or other trusted adult can help. Some people believe that the only way to deal with a bully is to stand up to the person, and they recommend responding to aggression with aggression. Others believe that fighting leads to more fighting and can make a sticky situation go from bad to worse. And what do you do if you are faced with anti-social behavior from an adult? There are no easy answers.

Even under the best of circumstances, with supportive peers and attentive adult allies sympathetic to your situation, confronting antisocial behavior is a challenge. Although the majority of those who are bullied keep it a secret, opening up about the experience can be extremely helpful to prevent damaging consequences for the victims. It is important for victims to understand that it is not their fault. Although it's not always possible to change the way that others behave, it is possible to learn to control your own reaction to others' antisocial behavior.

Self-Esteem

Self-esteem is a person's opinion of himself or herself. People who feel good about themselves have a high self-esteem; people who do not are said to have a low self-esteem. Being the target of antisocial behavior can lower one's self-esteem. Sometimes people faced with taunts, threats, and insults can start to feel like they deserve the treatment they're getting, even though nothing could be further from the truth. If you're a target, it's important to remember that no matter what people might say about you, or however they might treat you, it isn't your fault. It has nothing to do with you and everything to do with them. Try to stay strong and remember that when others hurt you, they are also hurting themselves.

It is important to maintain a strong sense of self—self-worth, self-esteem, and self-reliance—when you are the victim of antisocial behavior. Ultimately, it is the victimizers who have low self-esteem. Don't let them drag yours down.

Coping with Depression

According to the Johns Hopkins Bloomberg School of Public Health, 10 percent of young people undergo a traumatic emotional disturbance that greatly affects their home lives and academic performance. And according to a study by the *Journal of the American Academy of Child and Adolescent Psychiatry*, more than 8 percent of adolescents suffer from some form of depression. Depression can be very serious and can cause people to feel despair and lose perspective on their lives.

It can be hard to know what to do when one is feeling depressed. It is common for depressed people to want to sleep more than usual or suffer from insomnia. Depressed people are often listless (lacking in energy) and may have severely decreased appetites. Depression can impact people's schoolwork and their interpersonal relationships. Sometimes depression can manifest itself as anger or frustration, as well as substance abuse and risk taking behaviors. If you're feeling depressed, it doesn't just affect you. It also impacts everyone who cares about you.

Depression is more than the normal periods of sadness common in adolescence. It is deep and long-lasting, and can make its sufferers lose interest in the things they ordinarily love and the relationships they cherish.

Depression can be triggered by bad experiences and difficult situations, but it is also a result of brain chemistry. The presence or scarcity of certain chemicals in the brain creates the feeling of depression. Some people suffer from clinical depression, which means that they are chemically prone to feeling depressed even if everything is "fine" in their lives. But even those who don't suffer from clinical depression can feel depressed at times. The good news is, when you're feeling depressed, there are certain steps you can take to change your brain chemistry and change how you're feeling.

One of the oldest and most effective ways to treat depression is to talk to someone about it. This person could be a guidance counselor, a therapist, a trusted adult, or a perceptive friend. Talking about what's bothering you can help put things in perspective and help you move beyond unpleasant incidents.

One way to not deal with negative feelings is to take them out on other people. Lashing out at those who have done nothing wrong might be convenient, but it won't make anyone feel better, least of all yourself.

Dealing with Addiction

Substance abuse can be an antisocial behavior in that it drives a person's loved ones away and leads to poor decision-making. People who become addicted to drugs or alcohol often begin abusing them when they are still teenagers. This is a common age to begin experimenting with mind-altering substances. This is also the first time that teenagers will see their peers become addicted to drugs and alcohol.

Almost everyone who becomes addicted to a drug thinks that he or she can stop at any time, that it just takes willpower. But addiction is an extremely complicated phenomenon, and the millions of addicts around the world aren't simply people with poor willpower. Drugs and alcohol can change brain chemistry, making it so the brain connects substance abuse with happiness. Eventually, the brain can only associate happiness with substance abuse. Instead of feeling happy when something good happens, you can only feel happy when ingesting drugs or alcohol.

Such abuse can also interfere with crucial brain development during the teen years and lead to mental health issues later in life.

The best way to deal with addiction is prevention. Avoiding the temptations of drugs and alcohol will ensure that one will never become dependent on them. Beyond that, the most important way to stop addiction is to recognize when you, or someone you know, has a problem, and to get help. Substance abuse counselors are

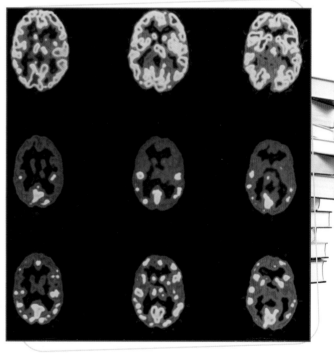

This MRI scan shows how cocaine use affects brain activity. The yellow and red colors indicate drug-fueled activity. Over time, damage to the brain can result.

29

trained to help people recover from addiction and figure out the best course of treatment. Sometimes that involves one-on-one counseling; often it involves group counseling and counseling with family members.

Being honest about one's problems can be difficult, and getting help can seem intimidating. This is completely natural and something that many people who need help struggle with. For many people, a stigma is connected to drug and alcohol use, and this stigma makes it difficult for them to seek help. However, seeking out a counselor or treatment program is undeniably the most effective way to combat addiction.

Again, it should be emphasized that addiction is a disease, and while many serious addicts will never be fully "cured," they can learn to manage their condition and live full, enriching, sober lives.

Reaching Out

For teens who are the victims of antisocial behavior, as well as for those who are struggling with antisocial urges, reaching out to others is crucial. Friends can provide an important support network, and you will probably find that many of your peers are going through the same things that you are. If you feel that you can't talk to members of your immediate family about what you're going through, members of one's extended family may be of help. Adult allies, such as teachers willing to lend a sympathetic ear, can give an insightful outside perspective on one's problems.

Your school guidance counselor can do more than just give you advice about classes or help you find a college.

Talking to a therapist, counselor, or other trusted adult about one's problems may be scary at first, but it can also be enormously helpful. You will feel relieved of a burden, and you will receive insightful advice.

He or she is also trained to help students deal with social and family pressures and give them—or direct them toward—help if they need it. Some teens are reluctant to get help because they worry that they'll be judged by their peers or they are afraid of their parents finding out. At the same time, they find that they are unable to deal with their problems by themselves.

Although it might not seem cool to talk to the guidance counselor, counselors are trained to help students who are facing problems at home or at school. Counselors can meet with students privately and have confidential

Being part of a positive support network is an enormous help when navigating the teen years. Friends can look after each other, band together, stick up for each other, and give and receive helpful advice in times of trouble.

conversations. Students who need help coping with antisocial behavior can talk to their counselor or they can request that their counselor refer them to someone who can provide additional help. For instance, a guidance counselor can refer students to mental health professionals who have experience working with students suffering from depression or other disorders. They can contact social workers, substance abuse counselors, and even family therapists.

Take Action: Looking Out for Friends and Peers

The friendship and support of one's peers is extremely important in the teen years, especially if one is the target of antisocial behavior. A key part of being a good friend is being there for your friends when they are the victims of antisocial behavior. This can be as simple as just listening to what they have to say, offering them advice, or inviting them to come hang out with you.

There are instances when you might know more about what your friends are going through than your teachers or even your friends' parents do. With this knowledge comes great responsibility; it's your job to look out for your friends' best interests. This involves more than just trying to cheer them up. If you notice that a friend has started bullying classmates, shoplifting, or getting into fights, let him or her know that you don't approve of these actions.

It is especially important to speak up if your friends begin using drugs and alcohol. Peer pressure is a huge motivating factor when it comes to teens beginning to experiment with drugs and alcohol, but peer pressure can work both ways. Research has shown that oftentimes people will base how frequently they engage in behaviors such as drinking on how frequently they think their peers are engaging in this behavior, or based on how much they think their friends and family approve of these behaviors. Rather than just sitting back while a friend begins abusing substances, speak up. Let your friend know that you value the friendship and that you aren't trying to be an authority figure or scold him or her, that you are speaking up because you are concerned for his or her well-being. Even if your friend doesn't listen to you right away, it is important that he or she hears what you have to say. It might make a big difference down the road.

MYTHS AND FACTS

Myth: If you're a minor, you can't get in any serious trouble with the law.

Fact: The justice system can prosecute minors as well as adults. Some juveniles are even charged as adults if the crime is seen as being serious enough. In addition, juvenile offenses can stay on one's criminal record.

Myth: There is nothing that teachers and school administrators can do to stop bullying.

Fact: It isn't always possible for teachers and school administrators to witness bullying when it occurs, but they are obligated to try and put a stop to bullying and harassment when they see it, suspect it, or receive a report about it.

Myth: No one can help you with your antisocial feelings.

Fact: Even if people at school don't understand you, or you feel like you can't speak with your parents, there are trained professionals who can help you. Your guidance counselor can tell you what your options are for professional help.

chapter four

Pushing Back: Combating Antisocial Behavior

In recent years, statistics have revealed just how widespread and serious antisocial behavior has become in the United States. In 2007, 2.8 million high school students reported that they had been pushed, tripped, or spat on, and 1.5 million high school students were threatened with violence.

Furthermore, some studies have suggested that as much as 70 percent of bullying is verbal. Verbal bullying may be harder for school officials to identify, and therefore can persist longer and escalate into other forms of bullying. This problem is even more acute for lesbian, gay, bisexual, and transgender (LGBT) students. According to a 2007 Gay, Lesbian, and Straight Education Network (GLSEN) survey, 90 percent of LGBT students reported that they were bullied at school, and more than 60 percent didn't feel safe at their school. In October 2010, the U.S. Department of Education sent a letter to administrators of schools around the country. The purpose of this letter

A sign posted outside an elementary school classroom in Georgia declares its zero-tolerance policy on bullying. Signs are posted throughout the school, and students are encouraged to report any bullying incidents.

was to remind the schools to obey their legal obligation to protect all their students from harassment.

Anti-Bullying Initiatives

Recognizing that bullying is a nationwide problem, the U.S. government created the Federal Partners in Bullying Prevention Steering Committee. The steering committee coordinates national anti-bullying resources and identifies areas where the government can allocate more resources. The committee has also launched BullyingInfo.org, a dedicated anti-bullying Web site. In addition, a bill pending in government, called the Safe Schools Improvement Act (SSIA), would require schools that receive federal funding to establish anti-bullying programs to protect students. SSIA would establish rules and guidelines about bullying prevention.

In the meantime, a number of local organizations and initiatives are taking on bullying in schools and providing outreach. A countless number of online resources have sprung up to help students no matter where they are in the country. One such online resource is the It Gets Better Project. Launched in response to a recent wave of suicides among bullying victims, It Gets Better consists of a series of online videos aimed at LGBT and other bullied teens. Grownups who have endured their share of mockery and misunderstanding and lived to tell the tale share their stories and promise kids that things will get better as they get older, often as soon as high school graduation. Many people have contributed videos to the project, including a number of celebrities and politicians. Even

President Barack Obama has filmed a video in support of this effort.

Stopping Substance Abuse

Beginning in 2007, the National Institute on Drug Abuse (NIDA) began Drug Facts Chat Day. Students can go online and ask NIDA scientists questions about drugs and drug use. Drug Facts Chat Day takes place during National Drug Facts Week. NIDA began this program in 2011 to dispel myths and provide students with solid facts on drugs. Programs like Drug Abuse Resistance Education (DARE) encourage students to officially pledge that they will avoid drugs and gangs. Students who participate in DARE are educated by actual law enforcement officers over a period of ten weeks about the dangers of drug use.

Mentoring Programs

Often antisocial behavior develops when teens begin hanging out with the wrong crowd. Other times, it's teens who don't have strong social ties, who aren't close to anyone, who act out. According to the Office of Juvenile Justice and Delinquency Prevention, in the twelve-to-fourteen age group, kids with no social ties and kids involved with antisocial friends are much more likely than their peers to engage in violence. It's important for teens to have someone responsible and trustworthy to connect with, trust, and look up to.

There are a number of programs in the United States that allow adults to mentor kids. One such organization is Big Brothers Big Sisters. This nonprofit is known for its effectiveness in making a positive impact on young people's lives. Adolescents who participate in the program are far less likely to engage in antisocial behaviors, such as experimenting with drugs and alcohol, committing violent acts, or failing to perform well in school. Founded in 1904, the organization now exists in twelve countries. Teens who suffer from the effects of antisocial behavior—both

Mentors can be invaluable guides when navigating the teen years. They can teach you how to avoid trouble, how to cope with problems, how to succeed in school and at work, and how to be a good and caring person.

as targets and as perpetrators—can benefit from mentoring of this kind.

In the end, our best tools to combat antisocial behavior are all social. Helping kids develop empathy, reach out to others, talk about their problems, and think through the consequences of their actions can free them from negative behaviors. After all, young people are still young. There's always a chance to grow, mature, heal, stop acting destructively, and build a positive future.

10 Great Questions to Ask a School Counselor

1. What should I do if I'm being bullied?

2. Will I get in trouble if I fight a bully?

3. What should I do if I am the target of cyberbullying?

4. Who can I talk to if my parents can't help me with my problems?

5. What should I do if I feel like I can't control my anger?

6. How much trouble can I really get into for vandalizing private property?

7. What should I do if a friend is using drugs or alcohol?

8. What is the school's responsibility to stop physical or emotional abuse of students by students?

9. Should I try to protect a friend who may be targeted for violent assault?

10. Can the school refer me to a therapist, and if so, will my parents be notified?

addiction A dependence, whether physical, psychological, or both, upon a certain substance or activity.

adrenaline A neurotransmitter that increases a person's blood flow and otherwise prepares him or her to respond to a real or perceived threat.

aggression The practice of engaging in activities that are intended to provoke or harm other people.

ally Someone who supports or sympathizes with another.

assault An attack that is either physical or verbal.

attention deficit/hyperactivity disorder (ADHD) A common behavioral disorder that affects both children and adults.

bullying Abuse, whether physical, emotional, or verbal, that takes place over a period of time.

depression A disorder that affects a person's sleep, appetite, and mood.

empathy The act of being able to identify with or sympathize with others.

exertion A sustained effort.

graffiti Images or writing that are painted or drawn on a wall; graffiti is common all over the world.

ostracize To exclude someone from a group, society, friendship, conversation, privileges, etc.

peer A person of one's own age, status, or social group.

stress A state of emotional worry, strain, or tension.

therapist A person who is trained to help others with emotional issues.

vandalism The act of wantonly destroying or damaging property.

Al-Anon/Alateen
1600 Corporate Landing Parkway
Virginia Beach, VA 23454–5617
(757) 563-1600
Web site: http://www.al-anon.alateen.org
This is a twelve-step group for the families and friends
of alcoholics and drug addicts. Alateen is specifically
for teenagers.

Big Brothers Big Sisters of Canada
3228 South Service Road, Suite 113E
Burlington, ON L7N 3H9
Canada
(905) 639-0461
Web site: http://www.bigbrothersbigsisters.ca
This is Canada's foremost mentoring program.

Canadian Centre on Substance Abuse
75 Albert Street, Suite 500
Ottawa, ON K1P 5E7
Canada
(613) 235-4048
Website: http://www.ccsa.ca
The Canadian Centre on Substance Abuse provides
information and leadership aimed at reducing substance abuse.

Gay, Lesbian, and Straight Education Network (GLSEN)
90 Broad Street, 2nd Floor
New York, NY 10004
(212) 727-0135

Web site: http://www.glsen.org
GLSEN is the leading national education organization
    focused on ensuring safe schools for all students.

National Association of Students Against Violence
    Everywhere (SAVE)
322 Chapanoke Road, Suite 110
Raleigh, NC 27603
(866) 343-SAVE (7283)
Web site: http://www.nationalsave.org
This student-initiated program promotes nonviolence
    in schools.

National Gang Center
Institute for Intergovernmental Research
P.O. Box 12729
Tallahassee, FL 32317
(850) 385-0600
Web site: http://www.nationalgangcenter.gov
This organization provides resources and information
    about gangs.

Office of Juvenile Justice and Delinquency Prevention
U.S. Department of Justice
810 7th Street NW
Washington, DC 20531
(202) 307–5911
Web site: http://www.ojjdp.gov
Dedicated to preventing juvenile delinquency, this organi-
    zation works to help local communities implement
    positive youth programs.

Stop Bullying Now! Campaign
U.S. Department of Health and Human Services
5600 Fishers Lane
Rockville, MD 20857
(888) ASK-HRSA (275-4772)
Web site: http://www.stopbullyingnow.hrsa.gov/kids
The Web site for the Stop Bullying Now! Campaign
    includes resources about bullying awareness, preven-
    tion, and intervention.

Students Against Destructive Decisions (SADD)
255 Main Street, Room 208
Marlborough, MA 01752
(877) 723-3462
Web site: http://www.sadd.org
SADD works to prevent teens from making destructive
    decisions.

Web Sites

Due to the changing nature of Internet links, Rosen
Publishing has developed an online list of Web sites
related to the subject of this book. This site is updated
regularly. Please use this link to access the list:

http://www.rosenlinks.com/tmh/anti

Biegel, Gina M. *The Stress Reduction Workbook for Teens: Mindfulness Skills to Help You Deal with Stress.* Oakland, CA: Instant Help Books, 2009.

Breguet, Teri. *Frequently Asked Questions About Cyberbullying.* New York, NY: Rosen Publishing, 2007.

Byers, Ann. *Frequently Asked Questions About Gangs and Urban Violence.* New York, NY: Rosen Publishing, 2011.

Coloroso, Barbara. *The Bully, the Bullied, and the Bystander: From Preschool to High School—How Parents and Teachers Can Help Break the Cycle.* New York, NY: Harper, 2009.

Edelfield, Bruce, and Tracey J. Moosa. *Drug Abuse* (Teen Mental Health). New York, NY: Rosen Publishing, 2011.

Gass, Justin T. *Understanding Drugs: Alcohol.* New York, NY: Chelsea House, 2010.

Hinduja, Sameer, and Justin W. Patchin. *Bullying Beyond the Schoolyard: Preventing and Responding to Cyberbullying.* Thousand Oaks, CA: Corwin Press, 2008.

Juzwiak, Rich. *Addictive Personality.* New York, NY: Rosen Publishing, 2008.

Kohut, Margaret R. *The Complete Guide to Understanding, Controlling, and Stopping Bullies & Bullying: A Complete Guide for Teachers & Parents.* Ocala, FL: Atlantic Publishing Group, 2007.

Levin, Judith. *Depression and Mood Disorders.* New York, NY: Rosen Publishing, 2008.

Lohmann, Raychelle Cassada. *The Anger Workbook for Teens: Activities to Help You Deal with*

Anger and Frustration. Oakland, CA: Instant Help Books, 2009.

Murphy, Alexa Gordon, ed. *Dealing with Bullying*. New York, NY: Chelsea House, 2009.

Peirce, Jeremy L. *Attention-Deficit/Hyperactivity Disorder*. New York, NY: Chelsea House, 2007.

Quill, Charlie. *Anger and Anger Management*. New York, NY: Rosen Publishing, 2008.

Rogers, Vanessa. *Cyberbullying: Activities to Help Children and Teens Stay Safe in a Texting, Twittering, Social Networking World*. London, England: Jessica Kingsley Publishers, 2010.

Wiseman, Rosalind. *Boys, Girls and Other Hazardous Materials*. New York, NY: Putnam, 2010.

Wiseman, Rosalind. *Queen Bees and Wannabes: Helping Your Daughter Survive Cliques, Gossip, Boyfriends, and the New Realities of Girl World*. New York, NY: Three Rivers Press, 2009.

About the Author

Frank Spalding is a writer living in New York City. He has written a number of books for Rosen Publishing. He has had a long-standing interest in criminal justice and anti-violence initiatives.

Photo Credits